EGYPTIAN BOATS

by **GEOFFREY SCOTT**
pictures by **NANCY L. CARLSON**

Carolrhoda Books
Minneapolis, Minnesota

for Kathy

LIBRARY OF CONGRESS CATALOGING IN PUBLICATION DATA

Scott, Geoffrey, 1952—
Egyptian boats.

(A Carolrhoda on my own book)
SUMMARY: Describes the various boats used in
ancient Egypt.

1. Ships, Wooden—Juvenile literature. 2. Shipbuilding
—Egypt—History—Juvenile literature.   3. Boats and
boating—Egypt—History—Juvenile literature. [1. Boats
and boating—Egypt—History. 2. Shipbuilding—Egypt
—History. 3. Egypt—Civilization] I. Carlson, Nancy L.
II. Title.

VM16.S36   387.2'1   80-27676
ISBN 0-87614-138-6

2   3   4   5   6   7   8   9   10   86   85   84   83   82

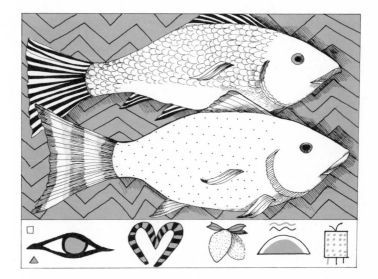

Over 4,000 years ago
people in Egypt asked,
"How does the sun move across the sky?"
The answer they gave was,
"A boat carries it."
That answer seemed good
because boats were so important to them.
The Egyptians lived along a river.
That river is called the Nile.
It's an important river today.
It was even more important long ago.

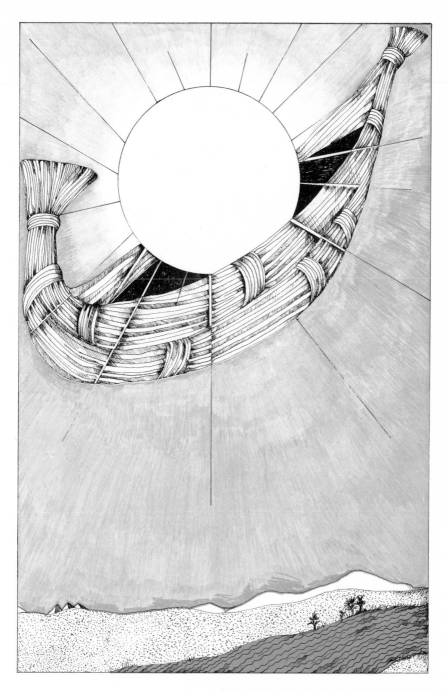

Let's go back in time 4,000 years.

If we stood on the banks of the Nile,

what would we see?

Look along the river's edge.

There is a small boat.

It looks a little like a canoe.

It's almost hidden by the tall reeds.

The man in it is hunting.

Farther out from shore
we see a long wooden boat.
That's the king's messenger boat.
It's full of soldiers.

The messenger boat quickly passes
a reed boat with a big white sail.
On the deck under the sail
are baskets of grain and jars of oils.

Now look in the middle of the river.

There is a big barge (barj).

The smaller boats are pulling it.

It's carrying cattle.

What a noise they make!

That funeral boat had better stay

out of the barge's way!

All the boats we saw on the Nile
were working.
They were carrying food and animals
from the country to the city.
They were carrying information
to Egypt's king.
They were carrying dead people
to their tombs.
Boats did a lot of work for the Egyptians.
No wonder they believed the sun
needed a boat too!

Let's look more closely
at some Egyptian boats.
The smallest boat on the river
was also the oldest.
It was called an ambatch (AM-bach).

An ambatch was the first Egyptian boat
ever made.
No one knows exactly when
the first ambatch was built.
But a good guess might be 6,500 years ago.

The early Egyptians knew
that wood floats well.
They knew it would make good boats.
But few trees grew in Egypt.
Not many boats could be made of wood.
The Egyptians had a problem.
What could they build their boats with?
Their answer was a long, thin plant
called a reed.
Reeds grew near the shore.
They grew all along the Nile.
The Egyptians saw that one reed floated.
Maybe many reeds tied together
would let a person float.

The ambatch was made of
two bundles of reeds.
They were tied together at the ends.
In the middle,
they were pushed apart enough
to let a person sit between them.

A reed mat was tied between the bundles

to make a floor.

When it was finished,

the ambatch looked like a small canoe.

It was a simple little boat.

One person could paddle it.

Ambatches made good boats for hunting.
People paddled them near the shore.
They caught the animals that lived there.
Ambatches were also used
to collect more reeds.
The reeds could be used
to build other ambatches.
Or they could be used
to make a kind of paper.
These ambatches worked very well.
In fact, they still do.
Boats like them are still used
on parts of the Nile today.
That's over 6,000 years
after they were first made!

21

Bigger, stronger boats were made
with larger, longer reed bundles.
This is a reed boat like the ambatch.
But it's much bigger.
This boat had six paddlers.
It also had a sail.
When the wind blew,
the sail could push the boat.
The sail was tied to a tall pole
called a mast.
The mast was held up by ropes
tied to the side of the boat.
Sailboats needed extra-thick floors
to hold the masts.

Those strong floors also made sailboats
able to carry more.
But bigger, heavier boats like this
needed people to steer them.
So two men stood in the back of the boat.
They steered it with big paddles.
Other men held ropes tied to the sail.
They turned the sail to catch the wind.

As time passed, Egypt grew.

There was wood on some of its new land.

Egypt also began to get wood

from its neighbors.

The Egyptians sold gold and food.

In return, they got wood.

Of course, more boats were needed

to carry all these things.

Bigger boats too.

But boats could now be made of wood.

Here is a boat made of wood.
It was called a
merchantman (MUR-chunt-man).
Merchantmen were big.
They were strong.
They could carry more than reed boats.
And because they were made of wood,
they lasted longer than reed boats.

Merchantmen didn't have paddles.

They had oars instead.

Oars are longer than paddles.

People who work them are called rowers.

Today we sit down when we row.

The Egyptians rowed differently.

First they stood up.

Then they put the oar into the water.

Next they pulled back on the oar

and sat down at the same time.

They looked like they were falling down

onto their benches.

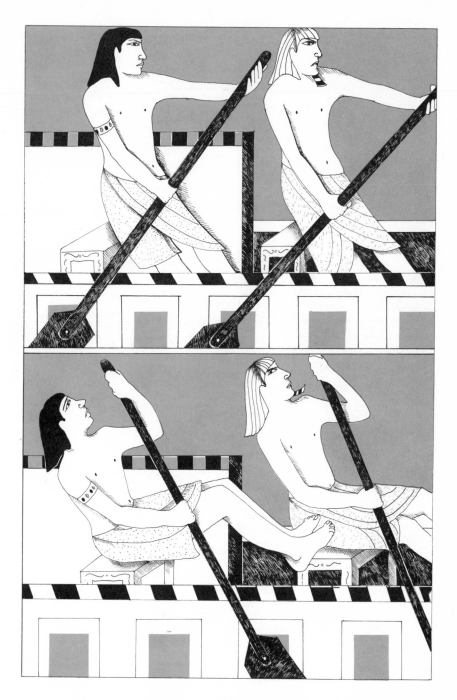

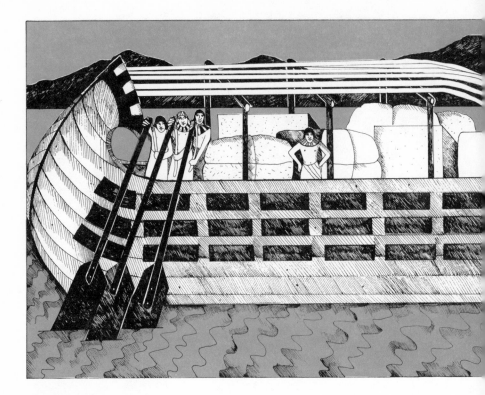

One boat on the Nile
made the others look like toys.
It was the barge.
Some barges carried animals.
Others carried stones for building.

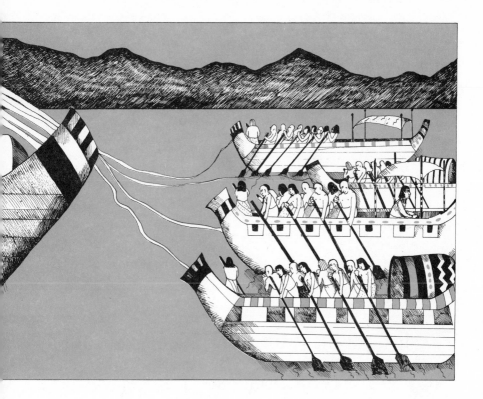

Barges had no sails or oars.

They had to be pulled.

Small boats pulled them.

A rope tied each small boat to the barge.

Slaves rowed the small boats.

And the barge moved slowly up the Nile.

Barges were made of wood.

But they were made very much like
the reed boats.

Today boats have a strong piece of wood
along the middle of their bottoms.

We call this piece of wood a keel.

It makes our boats strong.

The Egyptians didn't know about keels.

They made their boats strong
another way.

They tied big ropes from one end
of the barge to the other.

The ropes ran along the top of the barge.

They held the ends up.

They also made the barge stronger.

Important people often traveled in boats.

The king, for example.

We would be able to spot his boat quickly.

It was beautifully painted

with many designs.

Sometimes the designs told stories.

On the king's boat,

a piece of cloth hung on poles.

The king sat under it.

He stayed out of the hot sun.

There were many servants on the boat.

They prepared the king's food.

They waved fans to keep him cool.

Other boats followed the king's boat.

They carried soldiers to protect the king.

They carried men

to help him make decisions.

Sometimes messenger boats

came to the king's boat.

The messenger gave the king a message.

He got the king's answer.

Then he left quickly.

The king ruled his country

even from his boat!

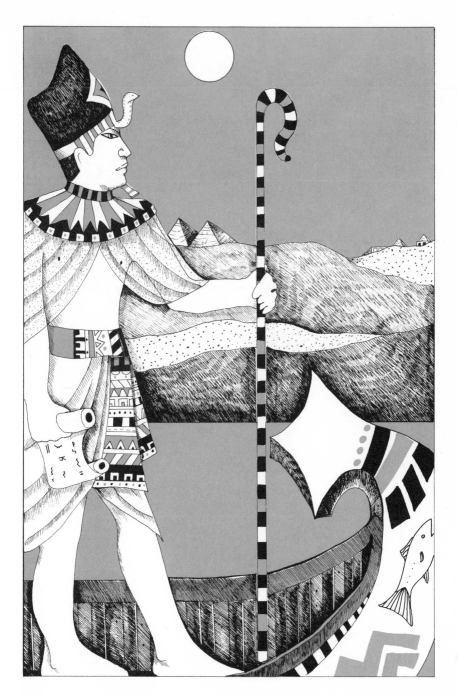

Egyptian funeral boats
carried mummies to their tombs.
The boats were painted like the mummies.
They had pictures of plants, animals,
and people on them.

Egyptians thought these pictures
had magic powers.
They would help the dead person
come back to life.
They called this the Life After Death.
The person would need food
in the Life After Death.
So the boat carried boxes of food.
Chairs, beds, shoes, and jewels
were carried along too.
If the dead person was important,
there might be many funeral boats.
Boats were important to the Egyptians
even after they died!

The Egyptians believed that the sun
sailed across the sky in a boat.
Their sun god, Ra (rah),
traveled in the boat with the sun.
Important Egyptians, like King
Tutankhamon (TOOT-ahngk-AH-mun),
wanted to sail with Ra
in the Life After Death.
So King Tut was buried with many boats.
These were not real boats.
They were models.
They were carefully put into Tut's tomb.
They all pointed west.
This gave the model boats
magic power to carry Tut.

The Egyptian boats we have seen

are not sailed much today.

Now there are modern boats on the Nile.

But a few years ago,

a man named Thor Heyerdahl (HI-ur-dahl)

had an idea about Egyptian boats.

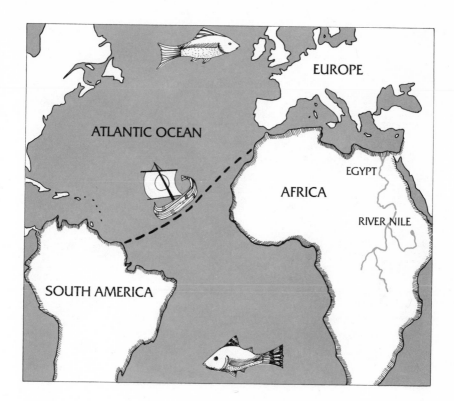

He thought they were very strong.

Strong enough to sail great distances.

Heyerdahl asked, "Could the Egyptians
have visited South America in their boats?"
To find out, he built a reed boat.
He named it *Ra.*

Ra carried seven men.

They set sail from Africa

to cross the Atlantic Ocean.

And they almost made it.

Ra fell apart just short of its goal.

But Heyerdahl didn't give up.

He tried again.

He built another boat.

It was called *Ra II*.

This time he made it!

He sailed across the Atlantic Ocean

in an Egyptian reed boat!

Heyerdahl was right.

Egyptian boats *were* strong enough

to sail across the ocean.

And think of all the jobs they did.

Is it any wonder then

that boats were so important

to the Egyptians—in life and death!

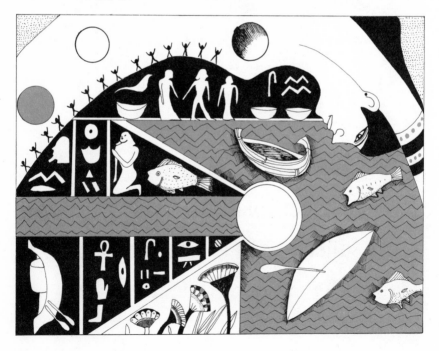